MIGRATION IN THE 21ST CENTURY

How will globalization and climate change affect
human migration and settlement?

By Paul Challen

Crabtree Publishing Company

www.crabtreebooks.com

Author: Paul Challen
Project director: Ruth Owen
Designer: Elaine Wilkinson
Editors: Mark Sachner, Lynn Peppas
Editorial director: Kathy Middleton
Prepress technician: Katherine Berti
Production coordinator: Margaret Amy Salter
Consultant: Ceri Oeppen BSc, MSc, of the Sussex Centre for Migration Research

Developed & Created for Crabtree Publishing Company by Ruby Tuesday Books Ltd

Front cover (top): Residents of New Orleans walk from floodwaters caused by Hurricane Katrina in 2005.
Front cover (bottom left): Many migrants arrive from rural areas to India's newly industrialized cities and end up living in slums when they are unable to find work.
Front cover (bottom center): Carbon emissions from factories add to the crisis of global warming.
Front cover (bottom right): In the United States, Canada, and the United Kingdom over a quarter of all medical professionals are immigrants.
Back cover: A young worker in a textile factory in India; many globalized companies take advantage of low pay rates and under-age workers in developing countries.
Title page: Refugees from Darfur at the Farchana Refugee Camp in Chad line up from early in the morning to collect water from stand pipes provided by aid workers. Over 18,000 people live in the camp and water supplies are always low.

Photo credits:
Alamy: page 12
Corbis: Jason Reed: front cover (top); Richard Wainwright: page 1; Zhou Hua: page 8 (top); Brooks Kraft: pages 9 (top), 14; Michael Reynolds: page 17 (bottom); Jagadeesh: pages 20–21 (center); Brian Lee: page 21 (top); Andrew Holbrooke: page 22 (bottom); Pallava Bagla: page 24; Carlos Barria: page 30 (bottom); David J. Phillip: page 31 (top); Romeo Ranoco: page 32 (left); Richard Wainwright: pages 34–35 (center); Ryan Pyle: pages 36–37 (center top); Richard Cannon: page 39; Ashley Cooper: pages 40–41 (center); Gideon Mendel: page 42
Cosmographics: page 35 (top)
Getty Images: Saul Loeb: pages 7 (bottom), 26 (bottom), 27 (all), 29 (top), 33; Yoshikazu Tsuno: pages 38 (bottom), 41 (bottom)
The Granger Collection: page 10 (bottom)
Library of Congress: page 13
NASA: page 28 (bottom)
Ruby Tuesday Books Ltd: pages 11 (top), 34 (top)
Shutterstock: front cover (bottom left, center, bottom right), back cover, pages 3, 4 (left), 5, 6, 7 (top), 8–9 (center), 10 (left), 11 (bottom), 16, 17 (top right), 18–19, 20 (top all), 22–23 (top center all), 22 (center right), 23, 26 (left all), 28 (top all), 29 (bottom), 36 (top left), 36–37 (bottom center), 37 (top right), 38 (left all), 40 (bottom), 43
Wikipedia (public domain): pages 4 (bottom), 15

Library and Archives Canada Cataloguing in Publication

Challen, Paul, 1967-
Migration in the 21st century : how will globalization and climate change affect migration and settlement? / Paul Challen.

(Investigating human migration & settlement)
Includes index.
ISBN 978-0-7787-5181-6 (bound).--ISBN 978-0-7787-5196-0 (pbk.)

1. Emigration and immigration--Forecasting--Juvenile literature.
2. Emigration and immigration--Economic aspects--Juvenile literature.
3. Globalization--Juvenile literature. I. Title. II. Series: Investigating human migration & settlement

GN370.C43 2010   j304.8   C2009-905267-9

Library of Congress Cataloging-in-Publication Data

Challen, Paul C. (Paul Clarence), 1967-
Migration in the 21st century: how will globalization and climate change affect migration and settlement? / By Paul Challen.
p. cm. -- (Investigating human migration & settlement)
Includes index.
ISBN 978-0-7787-5196-0 (pbk. : alk. paper) -- ISBN 978-0-7787-5181-6 (reinforced library binding : alk. paper)
1. Human beings--Migration--Juvenile literature. 2. Human settlements--Juvenile literature. 3. Emigration and immigration--Juvenile literature. 4. Globalization--Juvenile literature. I. Title.
GN370.C44 2010
304.8--dc22

2009034890

Crabtree Publishing Company

www.crabtreebooks.com   1-800-387-7650   Printed in China/122009/CT20090915

Published in Canada
Crabtree Publishing
616 Welland Ave.
St. Catharines, ON
L2M 5V6

Published in the United States
Crabtree Publishing
PMB 59051
350 Fifth Avenue, 59th Floor
New York, New York 10118

Published in the United Kingdom
Crabtree Publishing
Maritime House
Basin Road North, Hove
BN41 1WR

Published in Australia
Crabtree Publishing
386 Mt. Alexander Rd.
Ascot Vale (Melbourne)
VIC 3032

CONTENTS

CHAPTER ONE

LOOKING INTO THE FUTURE

Throughout history, there have been many reasons why people around the world have migrated to new locations. People have migrated to escape war or persecution. They have migrated to obtain land or to find employment. In the future, two of the most important factors causing people to migrate in large numbers will likely be globalization and climate change. This book will look at what these terms mean and how these factors will have a great impact on human migration in the years to come.

What Is Economic Globalization?

Globalization is the growth of something—trade and transportation are two examples—on a worldwide scale. Many companies start out by selling their products within their own region or their own country. Over time,

▲ Two instantly recognizable global brands—KFC and Domino's Pizza—doing business in Kolkata in India.

▲ *Globalized companies face all kinds of challenges when they expand into other countries to do business. They may have to develop new pizza toppings, for example, to sell in a Middle Eastern country where a topping such as sausage is forbidden. Or they might have to design a keyboard, like this English/Arabic computer keyboard, for people who speak a different language.*

some of these companies may begin selling to customers in other countries around the world. When that happens, these companies are said to be internationalizing their companies.

If a company then begins manufacturing its goods overseas and hiring people to work for it in countries around the world, the company is said to be globalizing its business. The Nike shoe and clothing company began life in the United States and in its first years manufactured most of its products there. Nike products were soon available in many countries around the world, and over time, Nike expanded its production facilities to other countries, such as China, Taiwan, India, Malaysia, and the Philippines. Today, Nike is said to have a "globalized" labor force. McDonald's is another company that started life in the United States and now has restaurants and workforces in 119 countries around the world.

In the late 1980s and early 1990s, globalization became more and more widespread. Companies began to realize that there was a worldwide market for their products and also opportunities to manufacture overseas and carry out other aspects of their business from a base in another country.

GLOBALIZATION AND CONSUMER POWER

Large companies that "go global" may expand their business into areas where they can pay workers less than they would at home. In some cases, those underpaid workers are children who are working to help their families afford food and housing.

Many consumers are not happy when they find out that products are being made by children or underpaid workers. Sometimes they will organize a "boycott" — they will tell others not to buy that company's products until the unfair treatment of workers has been stopped.

In the central Asian country of Uzbekistan, investigators from the World Fair Trade Organization (WFTO) found that up to 50 percent of the people picking cotton were under 16, and were actually being removed by force from school to pick cotton, often for up to 11 hours a day.

In early 2009, the WFTO urged people around the world to stop buying cotton produced in this way. Companies such as the retail chains Tesco, Wal-Mart, and Gap, all announced that they would no longer be selling Uzbek-grown cotton products.

▲ *Huge chunks of ice crash into the sea from a glacier in Antarctica. The increase in temperatures due to global warming is causing glaciers and the polar ice caps to melt adding extra water to the world's oceans, while the seawater itself is expanding as it gets warmer. In some places the level of the ocean has risen by 10 inches (25 cm) in the past one hundred years.*

What is Causing Our Climate To Change?

Over the last several decades, scientists have noticed that temperatures on our planet have been slowly rising. This gradual warming has become known as "global warming." Most scientists believe this warming is being caused by the burning of fossil fuels, such as oil and coal. When oil is burned to power a car or coal is burned to make electricity, it releases carbon dioxide, nitrous oxide, methane, and other gases into the atmosphere. These gases have become known as "greenhouse gases" because they trap the heat that rises from the planet's surface inside Earth's atmosphere, just like a greenhouse traps the Sun's heat. In the right amounts, these gases help sustain animal and plant life on Earth by holding just the right amount of heat in the atmosphere. However, too much heat is now being trapped, and it is causing our climate to change.

Even small increases in Earth's air temperature can have very serious results. The water levels of the seas, oceans, and rivers are already rising as glaciers and the polar ice caps are melting. In some parts of the world, droughts and heat waves are occurring. Extreme weather events, such as hurricanes and severe storms, will also become more frequent.

CLIMATE CHANGE AND CONSUMER POWER

▲ When drought occurs people cannot grow crops and they may eventually not have enough drinking water. Livestock will die from a lack of food and water, as will wild animals in the area. Here, zebras look for grass and plants to graze on in a dry, dusty landscape.

A Serious Problem

Over the last few decades, people around the world have become concerned about global warming and the resulting climate change—especially since this is largely a human-made problem. Since the development of factories in the 1800s and the mass production of automobiles in the early 1900s, the creation of greenhouse gases has been increasing, and the problem has become more and more serious.

One example of a consumer boycott that was launched because of environmental factors is the Tar Sands Boycott, organized by *Ethical Consumer* magazine. This boycott is aimed against the extraction of oil from a huge chunk of land around Fort McMurray, Alberta, Canada. This land contains sand that is rich in oil, but *Ethical Consumer* says that putting this much oil into production will raise carbon dioxide levels around the world to "catastrophic" levels.

To oppose the Tar Sands extraction, the magazine's Web site has published a list of the top ten companies that will profit from the extraction including Hitachi, Barclays Bank, and Koch Industries, a company that makes lycra for exercise clothing.

◄ Environmental protestors from the groups Oil Change International and ForestEthics demonstrate outside the Canadian Embassy in Washington, D.C., in 2008. The groups say the processes used to extract petroleum from the Alberta Tar Sands produce three times as many greenhouse gases as conventional oil production methods.

Combating Climate Change

Today, countries around the world are addressing climate change in a number of ways, all based on reducing the levels of greenhouse gases produced by our homes, industries, and transportation. U.S. President Barack Obama has committed his administration to developing programs that will reduce carbon dioxide emissions in the United States by 80 percent by 2050.

The solutions are not always simple. Countries such as China and India are often accused by people in the West of trying so hard to catch up with production levels in North America and Europe that they fail to control the enormous amount of pollution they are creating. Developing countries argue that they are simply using the same practices that countries in the

▲ ▶ *The economies of both India and China are growing fast, as are the number of factories and other industrial plants in both countries. Above, a vast oil refinery, newly opened in 2009, in the southwest of China will turn crude oil into gasoline, diesel, oil, plastics, and other petrochemical products. Right—Auto workers build cars in a factory in India.*

West used to build up their own economies 20 or 30 years ago—before many environmental regulations came into play in places such as the United States and the United Kingdom.

▲ *U.S. President Barack Obama has pledged $150 billion to developing energy-efficient technologies. Here, he is signing an executive order on combating climate change in January 2009.*

Predictions: What Does the Future Hold?

People who study human migrations—such as those who work for international organizations such as the United Nations or the World Health Organization—often make predictions about how certain factors may affect how people move in large numbers. Globalization and climate change are two of these factors. Based on what they know about specific events that are happening now, such as what areas global companies are focusing on for their expansion or what parts of the world have been hit hard by weather disasters, these experts can predict many things about human migration patterns.

The following chapters will look at some of these predictions and why the experts are making them. Globalization and climate change will also be examined to see how they will affect human migration in the 21st century.

PREDICTING HUMAN MIGRATIONS

People who predict how humans will migrate use a number of tools to do this. One such tool is called a mathematical model. This tool is actually a computer program. The program takes a huge number of factors that can affect migration—such as climate, economic factors, changes in government, and many others—and creates a "model" from them that predicts patterns of where and when people will move around the globe.

One researcher, Joel E. Cohen of Rockefeller and Columbia Universities in the United States, began presenting an important new model in 2009. This model should help governments estimate which parts of the world will see large numbers of new arrivals, and which can expect to see their populations decline. Of course, mathematical models make no "guarantees"—they are just highly sophisticated predictions. But they do provide a "best guess" about future human migration patterns.

CHAPTER TWO
A HISTORY OF TRADE & MIGRATION

For thousands of years, people have traveled outside the boundaries of their homelands. Sometimes, the reason for these voyages was simply to explore what other lands and peoples existed "out there." Trade with a neighboring country has always been another important reason to travel to foreign lands.

Trade in Human History

Our interest in trading with one another is one of the most important aspects of our history as human beings. In fact, many historians believe that it is possible to understand human history by learning more about how we have traded with one another—which groups traded together and what goods they traded.

◀ ▲ *Spices, such as black pepper, cinnamon, cumin, and nutmeg were much sought-after luxury products in Europe during the Middle Ages. Merchants became rich bringing spices from Asia to Europe. Above, a camel caravan carries goods through the inhospitable Pamir Mountains in Afghanistan on a route used by traders for hundreds of years.*

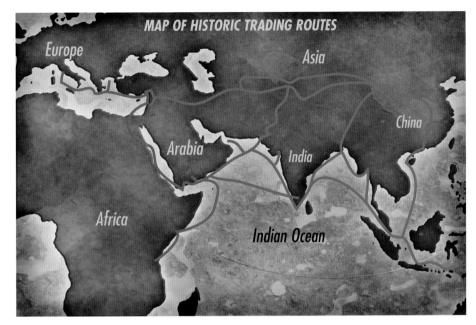

MAP OF HISTORIC TRADING ROUTES

Europe

Asia

China

Arabia

India

Africa

Indian Ocean

◀ *This map shows the land and sea routes taken by traders of spices and silks around 600 years ago.*

In the 1600s, for example, Europeans began to acquire a taste for coffee, which people in countries such as Egypt, Yemen, and Syria had been enjoying for several hundred years. The stories of Italian, Dutch, and French merchants, who traveled to what was then called "Arabia," describe how people in Europe were anxious to try this new beverage that kept them alert at night—and how Arabian merchants were interested in trading coffee for European goods as well.

Trade Routes

People's ability to travel has always had a major impact on trade. Covering large distances over land, by water, and, most recently by air, for the purpose of trade has created what are known as "trade routes." A trade route is a well-established path that people have used to get to places where they know they can buy, sell, and trade goods.

In the 1300s, a "spice route" was developed by spice traders who traveled to and from trading centers in Europe, Asia, and Africa.

Today, other routes have emerged, taking advantage of the speed and convenience of air travel. Many people in the banking industry, for example, journey from North American and European cities, such as New York or Amsterdam, to Asian financial capitals, such as Tokyo or Hong Kong, to conduct business several times a year. Airlines establish standard flying patterns that make this travel as quick and easy as possible.

▲ *Air travel means business people can attend a breakfast meeting in London, work on the plane for seven hours, and be in New York in time to meet clients for dinner!*

THE FUR TRADE

The North American fur trade in the 1600s and 1700s is an excellent example of the early roots of globalism and how trade affected human migration and interaction.

A European view: European explorers, farmers, and trappers all migrated to North America to take advantage of free land promised to them by their governments in England and France. They also sought to profit by trading furs with the Native people while building up settlements that would one day grow to large towns and cities. It was only over a period of time that Europeans became aware that their actions would harm Native people. By then, most Europeans felt it was time to open up North America in pursuit of economic interests that would justify the sacrifices being made by all, Native and European alike.

A Native view: Before Europeans arrived in the 1500s, indigenous people hunted, trapped, and grew crops. Although Native nations were sometimes in conflict, they generally lived in harmony with one another without developing large towns or cities as Europeans had. The arrival of Europeans led to the deaths of millions of Native people, either in war or through disease. Europeans, eager to acquire furs to sell back home, did not take Native people's well-being or economic needs into account in their interactions with them.

Trade in the New World: Migration in Action

The exploration of the so-called "New World" by Europeans beginning in the late 1400s is a good example of how global trade led to huge migrations of people. Early European explorers had reported that the lands we now know as North, Central, and South America were full of natural resources such as gold and silver, as well as new varieties of plants and wild animals.

Europeans began coming to the Americas in large numbers as the trade in goods such as lumber, beaver pelts, sugar cane, and cotton increased rapidly. And as more and more trade occurred, increasing numbers of Europeans migrated to the New World, pushed by poverty and the difficulty in owning land at home, and pulled by the promise of better opportunities to make a living and possess some land of their own.

Over time, this migration led to the development of towns and cities, industries, and, in general, a whole new way of life in the Americas. This increase in trade and the human migration that came with it had a profound effect on the people who lived in the Americas before Europeans arrived. Many Native groups in both North and South America found themselves in conflict with the migrating Europeans, who often used force to get the land—and the trade opportunities—they wanted.

▲ This woodcut illustration shows Tomo-Chi-Chi of the Yamacraws, a tribe of the Creek Indian Nation, trading furs with British General James Olglethorpe who founded the Georgia Colony.

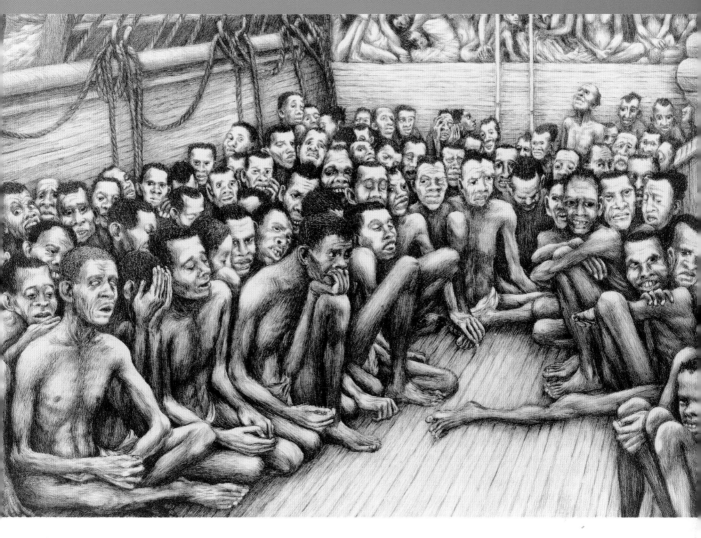

Slavery: Forced Migration for Global Trade

The slave trade in the Americas is an early example of how global economic forces grossly ignored human rights. Starting in the 1600s, large-scale farmers and plantation owners throughout the Americas began to realize that crops such as sugar cane and cotton could be grown and sold to Europeans at high prices. They also realized that these crops required a lot of labor to grow and harvest and that if such labor could be obtained cheaply, selling these crops would be a lot more profitable.

The answer to this need for cheap labor was to use slaves as the primary work force. Nearly all of the slaves who came to the Americas were from Africa, taken from their homelands by slave traders, sold to farmers, and then forced into providing unpaid labor. By the mid-1800s, slave trading and slavery itself had been banned throughout the Americas. In some countries, owners of the plantations where sugar and cotton were grown looked elsewhere for a supply of cheap labor to work in their fields, and many workers from China and other parts of Asia migrated to the Americas to do this.

▲ *It is estimated that over 10 million African people were taken from their homes and forced into slave labor in the Americas. This artwork by American artist Bernarda Bryson Shahn shows the horror of life onboard a slave ship bound for America. Male and female slaves, almost skeletal from lack of food, are crowded onto the deck of the ship.*

13

Global Trade Barriers . . .

Today, countries often place restrictions against other countries, making it difficult for the two to trade. For example, imagine a country where it is easy to hire car-factory workers at a low rate of pay and where cheap materials are used to make the cars those workers build. The low cost of labor and materials would mean that, overall, it would be cheap to build cars in that country.

Now, imagine another country where car-plant workers are well paid and where more expensive materials are used.

These plants are good for that country because they employ thousands of workers. But if cars from the first country are allowed to be shipped into the second country, they may be sold to people at a much lower cost than the ones made in the home country. And if people in the home country buy enough of the imported cars, its auto plants may be forced to close because nobody is buying the cars they are making. So the response of many countries in situations like this is to place what is called a "tariff" on the import of foreign products. That means that the makers of the foreign products have to pay a special tax to import them—driving the price up and making the home-made products still attractive to buyers.

In the 1980s in the United States, well-established automobile companies, such as General Motors and Chrysler, began to notice that Japanese auto makers Toyota and Honda were able to sell their vehicles in North America for prices that were, in many cases, lower than the North American manufacturers could charge. In addition, the Japanese firms had perfected the art of making small, fuel-efficient cars—not something seen before in the North American market. The result was that, at first, the

▲ Foreign-made automobiles are unloaded at the Dundalk Marine Terminal in Baltimore in 1971. The U.S. auto industry has been affected by the import of cheaper cars from overseas.

▲ ▼ In the 1980s, sporty or large American-made cars such as General Motor's Chevrolet Camaro (in blue) and Chrysler's Cordoba (in red) were suddenly competing against smaller, cheaper Japanese-made cars at home.

North American auto industry experienced a big drop in profits—meaning that thousands of auto workers lost their jobs. Over time, though, tariffs on Japanese autos were raised—while the North American manufacturers became better at making small, fuel-efficient cars to stay competitive.

JOURNEY STORIES

SELLING BOOKS WORLDWIDE:

The publishing industry is one of the most globalized industries in the world. A book may be written by an English author and published by a UK publishing company, but translated editions of that book will then be published around the world in other languages. For example, the Harry Potter books by British author J.K. Rowling have sold millions of copies to readers worldwide and have been translated into over 60 different languages. Susan is an international sales person for a UK publishing house. She travels to trade fairs around the world to meet with publishers from other countries:

Every year I travel to trade fairs where publishers from around the world meet to do business. The main trade fairs in the publishing industry are held in London in the UK, Frankfurt in Germany, Bologna in Italy, and major cities throughout the United States. I will attend the trade fair for several days and during that time I will meet with up to 50 publishers from other countries. I present the books that my company is producing to these foreign publishers, and if they like the book, they may buy it for their country. The foreign publisher will then translate the book into their language and sell it to consumers back home. It's exciting to see a book that your company has produced be translated into languages as diverse as Chinese, Hebrew, Russian, and even one time, Papiamento, for readers on the Caribbean island of Aruba.

FOCUS ON:

▲ The circle of gold stars on the flag of the European Union represents solidarity and harmony between the people of Europe.

THE EUROPEAN UNION

In addition to stimulating trade between European nations, the 27-member European Union (EU) makes it easier for citizens of EU countries to migrate to other EU nations by enforcing a directive (set of rules) that gives citizens "the right to move and reside freely within the Member States" while reducing "administrative formalities" such as filling out paperwork at border crossings.

▼ Citizens of the European Union member countries are also citizens of the European Union. This is shown on the cover of their passport.

MAP OF THE 27 EUROPEAN UNION MEMBER STATES

▼ The euro is a currency used by some of the European Union member states. The euro was introduced in 2002, and it replaced the countries' individual currencies. Use of the euro between the eurozone countries makes it easier for people and businesses to buy and sell things because they no longer have to convert between different currencies.

... and Trade Helpers

Sometimes, countries are able to come to agreements that actually encourage trade between them—instead of discouraging it by tariffs. Today, many countries in Europe encourage trade among themselves by working together within a group of countries called the European Union (EU). The EU enforces a number of policies and regulations that help its members trade profitably with one another as well as with countries outside the Union. As of 2009, the EU has 27 member nations. These nations depend heavily on one another as trading partners, and most of the countries share a common currency, the euro. Such a close group of trading partners is also unlikely to have another war like World War I or II, both of which started as conflicts between European nations.

Other groups that encourage trade among nations have global reach. The World Bank is an organization that lends money to poorer countries around the world so they can invest in ways that will help them gain ground on richer nations. The World Trade Organization acts as a kind of worldwide "watch dog" on tariffs, making sure countries do not take advantage of one another and stepping in to solve trade disagreements that arise.

NAFTA

The North American Free Trade Act (NAFTA) is an agreement between Canada, the United States, and Mexico. The agreement set up these three countries as a "free-trade zone" in which certain goods could move freely across borders of all three nations without the tariffs that existed before. When it was adopted in 1994, NAFTA became the largest free-trade zone in the world. The agreement has meant new opportunities for businesses, new customers for businesses in all three countries, and more choices for consumers living in the zone.

◄ Delegates attend the 79th meeting of the Development Committee at the World Bank headquarters in Washington, D.C., in April 2009. The Development Committee meets to discuss ways to assist the economies of developing countries.

Welcome

| lucts | About us | Forum | News |

Travel agency

The World
» Africa Hostels
» Asia Hostels
» Middle East Hostels
» Oceania Hostels
» Europe Hostels
» North & Central America Hostels
» South America Hostels

Airline Ticket	Amsterdam
Local Resources about	Bangkok
Airline Ticket	Beijing
	Frankfurt
	Hong Kong
	Johannesburg
	London
	Paris
	Rome
	Sydney

HOTEL
★★★★★

Top 20 Hotel and Hostel Destinations

Amsterdam	Dublin	Munich	Sydney
Athens	Edinburgh	New York City	Venice
Bangkok	Florence	Paris	
Barcelona	London	Prague	
Berlin	Madrid	Rome	
Chicago	Milan	Stockholm	

CHAPTER THREE

OUR GLOBAL WORLD

You have probably heard many people say that technology is making the world "smaller." What that means, in terms of globalization and migration, is simple. Two hundred years ago it would have taken weeks for a letter or person to travel to another country—today an email can arrive in seconds and a person in just hours.

▶ Today, we no longer need to travel for weeks or months to make a deal, or trade—we can buy, sell, and make a profit in just a few minutes using the telephone, email, or Internet. A manufacturer in China can do business with a customer in the United Kingdom without either party needing to leave their desk!

Opening a Window on the World

Two hundred years ago, it would have been impossible for most people to see what life was like in a new country before moving there. People could not really make any decisions about migrating some place and starting a new life there unless they traveled there themselves or exchanged information with someone who had been there. Today, that is made so much easier by technology. Through telephones, email, and the Internet, people around the world are able to know much more about the choices that await them if they are going to migrate.

Increasing the Pace Through Technology

Technology has also sped up the pace of globalization, making new types of work a possibility for people in developing countries such as India. In turn, the opportunity to do this work has driven people to migrate to where the jobs are. One example of this work is the outsourcing—the employing of another company to do work for you, often overseas—of word processing and graphic design work. Many office supply stores in North America and Europe offer a service in which people can have written documents such as letters or résumés professionally formatted and designed. This work is not done in the store, however. The work is sent via email to workers in India who do the formatting and design and then send the documents back. This type of business has led to the creation of new jobs in India that did not previously exist. Because the large offices specializing in this kind of service are usually sited in or close to cities, this employment opportunity has produced a sizeable migration from rural areas in India to urban areas.

◀ The globalization of communication technology has made it easier for migrants to keep in touch with their friends and family through email and webcams.

◀ In the United States, Canada, the United Kingdom, and New Zealand, over a quarter of all medical professionals are immigrants.

Global Trends

The previous chapter looked at how organizations such as the European Union are working to break down trade barriers. The rapid advancement of communications technology, such as the invention of email and cell phones, has also sped up the process of globalization, creating jobs and economic opportunity where none existed before. Here are some more examples of how economics, global workforces, and migration issues come together in a globalized world.

Migration and Health Care Workers

Almost every country has a system for training doctors, nurses, and other people who work in health care. The training is usually very difficult and takes a long time. But in some countries, such as Iran or Sudan, more trained doctors and nurses emerge from universities than there are jobs in hospitals and clinics for them to fill. Over the last two decades, many of these medical professionals have migrated to other countries, especially to Canada, the United States, and the United Kingdom.

Some medical workers may choose to migrate to benefit from higher pay overseas. This can benefit the migrant's home country, too, if they send remittances (money) home to their families. In some poor countries, such as the Philippines, the "export" of skilled workers is an industry in itself. More professionals are trained than are needed in the country as a deliberate strategy to increase the flow of foreign money back into the country in the form of migrant remittances and investment.

International Call Centers

Many businesses have a need to conduct business by telephone. Over the past ten years, many companies in North America and the United Kingdom have "outsourced" this telephone-based work to countries such as India or the Philippines because labor is cheaper there. In those nations, working as a telephone representative for a bank or credit card company is quite lucrative, so many well-educated workers have migrated to cities to work in these jobs. One 2004 survey showed that Indian

call center workers made an average of about $4,000 per year—compared to the average wage in their country of $2,000. The problem is that cities in places such as India are already very crowded, and a migration of call center workers makes this even worse.

In response to this problem some call center operators are now setting up these facilities in rural areas. In the rural district of Andrha Pradesh, the Byrraju Foundation, a group that specializes in "ruralizing" Indian call centers, is setting up centers that create jobs in rural areas to stop the migration of workers to crowded cities. This also brings much needed income to poor, rural towns and villages since the wages paid to rural workers as call center operatives are significantly higher than they could earn in other jobs outside big Indian cities.

◄ ▲ Top—Deepak Thampi teaches prospective Indian call center workers English grammar and pronunciation. Most Indian people speak English but to work in a call center they are taught to speak with an accent and in a style appropriate to the customer's country. Sometimes this includes adopting a new English- or American-sounding name. Left— Indian call center employees at work in Bangalore.

21

Irregular Migration

While it has become easier for money and products to cross borders, there has not been a corresponding effect for people crossing borders to work. Therefore, many migrant workers, known as irregular migrants, cross borders outside of authorized crossing points.

In richer countries such as the United States and Canada, the law requires that employers keep records on the workers they hire. These records must include how much employees are paid, what hours they work, and what safety conditions are being maintained on job sites. Irregular migrant workers often take jobs where employers break the law by not keeping these records. The employers save money by not paying irregular migrant workers medical benefits and by paying them less than local workers. They also get them to fill unsafe or difficult jobs that local workers are unwilling to do. Irregular migrant workers take these types of jobs because they do not have the right documents to get other jobs.

In the United States, this problem is particularly noticeable in the Southwest, where thousands of irregular immigrants enter the country from countries in Latin America, Mexico in particular. The governments of both countries are eager to stop this migration, but the sheer size of the U.S.-Mexico border and the large volume of irregular migration across it makes it very difficult to control.

Canada's Immigrant Labor Force

Compared to many countries around the world, Canada has a relatively "open" policy towards workers coming to fill jobs. In the earliest days of Canada's history, the government encouraged settlement from England and France as a way of filling the huge amount of open land available. This policy continued into the 1800s and 1900s as the nation's borders expanded to the west and

▼ ▶ *Right — A migrant worker from Mexico works over the border in a California vineyard. Bottom — Many Mexican families are split with some members living in Tijuana in Mexico and some in San Diego in the United States. They meet to talk and socialize through the border fence.*

people from Asia and Europe arrived in search of land and jobs.

The post-World War II era, after 1945, also saw tremendous growth in Canada's immigrant population, as people from all over the world came, once again, to fill jobs and land space. One notable example of this migrating labor force was the 500,000 Italian migrants, mostly from the south and central parts of Italy, that arrived in Canadian industrial centers from the 1950s through to the 1970s. The Italian migrants came to fill jobs in steel factories and associated heavy industries.

When Canadians are asked if migrant workers have been good for the country, the general public opinion is that they have—as compared to many countries in Europe, where there is considerable resentment against immigrant labor. Canada owes the vibrant, multicultural qualities of its society to immigrant groups from Italy, Portugal, China, and India (to name but a few) that have settled in large numbers in the country's main cities.

◀ *The United States-Mexico border fence looking from Tijuana into San Diego, and a road sign warning motorists to be aware of migrants on busy roads trying to cross the border.*

JOURNEY STORIES

NIMIT:

In 1984, Nimit and his family left Zambia in Africa and migrated to the United States. Nimit's father is from India and his mother is African.

My dad, Mahendra, was enjoying life as the owner of a successful clothing factory. However, after a series of robberies, and as more and more riots were occurring in Zambia, he decided to leave everything, and start a new life in America.

For the next six years, my parents worked various 9-5 jobs, including jobs at McDonald's and Burger King, and even worked night shifts at times. I would rarely see my parents in the same room at the same time, as one came home and the other went to work.

However, in 1994, my family finally saw the beginning of "easy street." My dad became a manager of a motel in Crystal City, Virginia, and soon thereafter, also became the manager of a motel in Alexandria, Virginia. Working both jobs, with the help of my mom, and to some extent me, the issue of money slowly disappeared. As a result, my dad was able to buy a hotel in Alabama. Simultaneously, he also began working on another project, building a hotel in Maryland. . .

My family knows that where we stand now is, by far, better than where we would stand in India, or even in Africa. When relatives hear of our opportunities and privileges, the freedom we have, and our stories of life in America, they want to move to America.

▼ In India many people are migrating from rural areas to cities hoping to find work that is better paid than rural jobs such as tea picking (bottom right). Unfortunately, when they arrive, many migrants cannot find a job in the city. With no money and no job, they are soon reduced to living in makeshift shelters in slum areas on the outskirts of the city.

Does Globalization Mean Equality?

Will globalization actually make countries around the world more equal in terms of their wealth and economic prosperity? After all, if the world is becoming one big, global "marketplace," people in countries that have traditionally been poorer should expect that they will be able to catch up, over time, to their global partners.

In reality, this has not always been the case, as market capital, money and goods, has not flowed back and forth freely. Workers in an Indian factory, for instance, may indeed be making more money than they could in other jobs in that country, but their wages are still relatively low compared to North American workers. This means that North American employers are saving a lot of money in labor costs, making big profits, and passing these profits on to their own communities through spending money locally, and not in India. The result is that the economic position of India does not benefit as much as that of the North American country.

Critics of globalization argue that along with new forms of industry and the promise of economic growth, western companies often "export" problems, such as excessive pollution and poor environmental practices, that may not have been seen before in developing countries. These countries may not be equipped to deal with carbon emissions, polluted water sources, or excessive waste from manufacturing, and these impacts may far outweigh the benefits brought by new jobs. Also, forms of manufacturing that are unfamiliar in a new country can bring about a whole host of safety problems because, while there has been a globalization of business, there has not been a globalization of labor laws.

Globalization's Downside: The Bhopal Disaster

In December 1984, the city of Bhopal, India, suffered perhaps the worst environmental disaster of all time—one that is still having an effect today. The Union Carbide chemical plant, half owned by the U.S. company of the same name, and half by Indian owners, was the site of a huge explosion. More than 40 tons (40 tonnes) of toxic gas was released into the air, with more than 500,000 people coming into direct contact with this poison.

It is estimated that within three days, almost 10,000 people died because of exposure to this gas. Since the disaster, a further 25,000 people have died, and up to 200,000 people are suffering permanent injuries. Decades later, people in the area continue to suffer from poor health because of the explosion.

Union Carbide has admitted very little responsibility in the Bhopal disaster, even though investigators have found much evidence of old, poorly maintained, and badly inspected equipment at the plant. Many have contended that the disaster never would have happened at a location in the United States or United Kingdom, because labor laws and practices would have ensured better conditions.

▼ *Dr. D.K. Satpathy stands with a collage commemorating the victims of the Bhopal disaster. Dr. Satpathy and his colleagues conducted over 2,500 post-mortems in three days following the Bhopal disaster.*

CHAPTER FOUR

OUR CHANGING CLIMATE

In the 1800s, developed nations such as Britain, the United States, and Germany underwent a change known as the "Industrial Revolution." Prior to that time, most people worked in rural areas or small villages, farming or making goods in small batches by hand.

Progress Has Its Price

In the late 1700s, advancements in technology made new machinery available that could mass produce goods. Soon, factories grew and industry became the main driver of many of these countries' economies and their main source of employment. The problem was, however, that with all this progress, it was easy to disregard the fact that factories had one side effect

▲ An industrial town in Yorkshire, England, in the 1950s. Smoke and pollution can be seen belching from the factory chimneys in the town.

◀ From the first steam trains to today's gasoline-powered family cars, methods of transportation that rely on fossil fuels have been polluting the air and causing global warming.

that farming and small manufacturing never had—pollution. Along with the enormous blast furnaces churning out steel came thick black clouds that people had never before seen—or been forced to breathe in. For almost a century—throughout the 1800s and into the early 1900s—people did not take the long-term effects of this pollution seriously—at least not seriously enough to curb industrial production to any great degree.

▲ *In 1913, American engineer and businessman Henry Ford invented the assembly line—an efficient way to make cars, lots of cars! Here Ford workers build cars at the Ford motor plant in Detroit.*

Planes, Trains, and Automobiles

Throughout the 1900s, science and technology made monumental advancements that were felt in many ways throughout the industrialized world. Alongside the new technologies needed to manufacture products out of steel, came more uses for steel. One of these uses—the automobile—was accelerated by the development of assembly-line production, which made it possible to produce more cars at cheaper prices. In addition to passenger cars came buses, trucks, military transports, racing cars, and motorcycles—all gasoline-powered and adding to pollution.

It took remarkably little time from the Wright Brothers' first engine-powered flight in 1903 for airplanes to fill the skies in times of both war and peace—again, powered by gasoline-fueled engines. Coal- and diesel-powered trains became increasingly in demand as ways of transporting people and goods long distances. To accommodate the increased need for all of these ways of getting places, more and more factories were built, with more machines requiring the generating of electricity to keep them running.

▲ *In just over a decade the aviation industry went from the first flight of an engine-powered plane to a sky filled with warplanes heading into battle during World War I.*

▲ The production of plastic products creates pollution and carbon emissions. When these products are thrown away, whether dumped as litter (seen here) or in landfills, they then take hundreds of years to biodegrade (rot away).

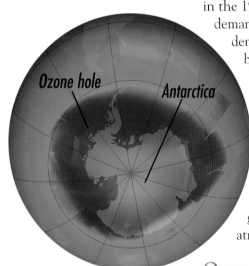

▲ Gases produced by industry can rise up and create holes in the part of Earth's atmosphere known as the ozone layer. This layer of gases is important because it prevents harmful rays from the Sun from hitting Earth's surface. Here, the vast ozone hole over Antarctica (as of June 2009) can be seen in blue.

Toys, Tubes, and Shaving Cream

The development of plastics for widespread commercial use hit its stride in the 1920s. With the development of plastics came an increased demand for plastic goods and an industry willing to satisfy that demand. Soon toy companies, furniture manufacturers, and other businesses were building factories and equipment to manufacture more and more products out of plastic.

By the 1940s, aerosol spray cans had been patented and were being put in use, first by soldiers in World War II as a means of dispensing insect repellant and eventually by just about everyone else to contain and deliver a variety of products, from deodorant, hair spray, and shaving cream to furniture polish, cooking oil, and air freshener. With the delivery of these commercial products also came the release of gases that would pollute the air we breathe, trap heat in Earth's atmosphere, and weaken our planet's protective ozone layer.

Opening Our Eyes to a Crisis

For most of the 1900s, as long as cars, chemicals, plastics and other products were being produced efficiently, it didn't seem important to consider the effects of industry on the environment. By the 1960s, however, people were starting to question whether all that pollution was harming our planet. One book, *Silent Spring*, by U.S. author Rachel Carson, published in 1962, got many people thinking about how chemicals used in agriculture were hurting the environment.

Today, our awareness of the effects of pollution on Earth's air, water, and land is extensive. It is understood that with increasing levels of greenhouse gases comes the trapping of heat in the atmosphere and warmer air temperatures. With higher temperatures come melting ice caps, rising water levels, flooding, and the possibility of increased—and increasingly severe—weather patterns and storm activity.

The Katrina Generation of Migrants

In August 2005, a huge storm hit the southern United States in the area around the Gulf of Mexico. Known as Hurricane Katrina, this storm caused the deaths of almost 2,000 people in sections of Florida, Alabama, Louisiana, and Mississippi, and about $81 billion in damages. Especially hard hit was the city of New Orleans, Louisiana.

▲ On April 3, 1963, writer and biologist Rachel Carson was interviewed for a CBS Reports TV program (seen here). Americans were shocked by Carson's research into the damage that chemical pesticides were doing to animals, plants, the soil, and even humans.

Hurricane Katrina was also significant in terms of human migration. Somewhere around 1.5 million people left the area in and around New Orleans because their homes, streets, and neighborhoods had been washed away by the initial storm or the flooding that followed. More than 300,000 of those people are expected never to return to New Orleans.

◄ Like so many tiny islands, flooded and abandoned homes around New Orleans stretch into the distance.

HURRICANE KATRINA: WHY DIDN'T EVERYONE EVACUATE?

As Katrina approached, why did some people stay?

In early 2009, a team of U.S. psychologists conducted surveys among two groups of survivors of Hurricane Katrina. One group fled New Orleans; the other chose to stay behind. Here are summaries of what the psychologists found in each group.

Stay: *This group described itself as feeling a strong sense of connection with their neighbors and community. Many also expressed a strong belief that a higher power (some described it as God) would take care of them. Some observers had thought that those who did not evacuate were either "lazy" or were overwhelmed by a feeling of "powerlessness." In reality, this group actually felt that their decision to stay and "tough it out" through the storm was a deliberate and reasonable choice of action based on their support and belief systems.*

Leave: *This group characterized itself as "action oriented" and unwilling to "let things happen"—they believed that the only correct course of action was to leave their homes and neighborhoods in order to avoid being killed. This was the group most praised by outside observers and responders— police, firefighters, rescue workers— for its decisive actions.*

Post-Katrina migrants settled all over the United States in a process that is considered the largest resettlement effort in U.S. history, both in terms of sheer numbers of people and the huge amounts of food, medical aid, and housing that were needed. Other cities absorbed many of these migrants. More than 35,000 refugees relocated to Houston, Texas, and tens of thousands more were added to the population rolls of other cities away from the Gulf coast in Louisiana to cities such as Mobile, Alabama, and Chicago, Illinois. Just after the resettlement began, Michael Chertoff, head of the U.S. Department of Homeland Security, the group mainly responsible for the resettlement, said, *"This is a tremendous . . . challenge. We are basically moving the city of New Orleans to other parts of the country."*

Will This Happen Again?

Many weather experts say that one of the results of global warming is that violent storms like hurricanes will continue to get worse. Unless something is done about greenhouse gases and the damage they are doing to the atmosphere, more severe storms like Katrina can be expected.

▲ *The Astrodome Stadium in Houston, Texas, became a temporary home to 16,000 people evacuated from the flooded city of New Orleans.*

New Orleans' location at the meeting place of land and two major bodies of water—the mouth of the Mississippi River and the Gulf of Mexico—puts it in a place where air currents would be especially active and likely to "feed" a major hurricane striking the area. In addition, the fact that so much of New Orleans lies below sea level makes it a prime candidate for the kind of flooding that Katrina spawned.

In this, New Orleans is not alone. Around the world, millions of people live in cities that are close to the ocean or rivers. They live below, level, or just above sea level. If sea levels continue to rise, and if more extreme weather events happen, these people will be in danger and may have to leave their homes.

▲ New Orleans residents are rescued from the roof of their home by helicopter.

JOURNEY STORIES

MELISSA:

Melissa was born in New Orleans and had lived there her entire life. When Hurricane Katrina hit, Melissa was living in a rented house with two other people in the area of the city called Lakeview:

Needless to say, we lost everything we ever had. The water was 9 feet (2.7 meters) high, up to the eve of the houses, and not much was able to be salvaged...

When my family and I left the day before the storm hit, I had $20 in my pocket.

We went to Shreveport first, then to Minden, then to Houston, then to Dallas. We came very close to living out of my car due to lack of accommodations. The worst feeling in the world is finding out that you are homeless and have nowhere to go. When we came back to our beloved home and neighborhood, it broke our hearts. Lakeview looked like some destroyed ghost town out of a horror movie. The trees were brown and decayed, the ground was covered with dirt and mud from the canal where the levees broke, the walls of our home were covered, and I mean covered, in black mold, the furniture was displaced, and it smelled of mildew. It was a nightmare...

CHAPTER FIVE

CLIMATE CHANGE: THE FUTURE

Scientists, politicians, economists, and many other experts continue to make predictions about how climate change will affect weather patterns—and how those patterns will have an impact on where people live and how and why they migrate.

Climate Migrants in the World Today

The United Nations University estimated that by 2008 there were 24 million migrants in the world—including up to 17 million Bangladeshis and four million Filipinos who have moved over the past several decades from low-lying areas for environmental reasons within their countries.

Climate change is expected to change weather patterns and living conditions, and may encourage more migration in the future and lead to the creation of many millions of new "climate migrants." There are two major ways that climate change will increase migration in the years to come: (1) the destruction of people's homes and elimination of jobs due to sudden and severe storms; and (2) the disappearance of land, water, and energy sources and the resulting conflicts arising over competition for these commodities.

In the Wake of Katrina

As was seen in the previous chapter, increasingly severe storms like Hurricane Katrina could destroy housing and jobs and encourage migration. Governments will work hard to ensure that hard-hit areas recover, but it is not always certain that people will be willing—or able—to return to their homelands after recovery efforts are complete.

◀ *Climate migrants in the Philippines walk along a flooded national highway after evacuating their houses that were hit by flashfloods caused by Typhoon Winnie in November 2004. Flashfloods occur when rain falls hard and fast, and the ground cannot soak it up quickly enough.*

▲ *In May 2009, Cyclone Aila slammed into the coast of Bangladesh causing a huge surge of ocean water which washed away villages and roads. Bangladesh regularly suffers devastating floods. Much of Bangladesh is just above sea level. The country also experiences annual monsoon rains (very heavy rains) and has four major rivers which bring huge quantities of water into the country.*

Fighting for Resources

The disappearance of land, water, and energy sources through global warming could lead to conflict and migration. Droughts and the rising level of waters around the world will mean that land for food crops may grow scarcer and scarcer, forcing people to fight for available land.

Take, for example, the conflict in the African nation of Sudan between the mostly Muslim and Arab government in the nation's north and the mostly Christian and African tribespeople struggling for survival and equal treatment in the south. This conflict has been ongoing since the 1950s, and in recent times has centered on the region of Darfur in western Sudan. Here, between 200,000 and 500,000 people have been killed and more than two million have been displaced as refugees.

FORCED CLIMATE MIGRATION IN A NATIVE ALASKA VILLAGE

At least one coastal village in western Alaska has felt the sting of global warming in a way that some scientists predict will become increasingly common over the next few decades. The 340 Yup'ik residents of the village of Newtok have voted to move their community nine miles (14.5 km) to higher ground up the Ninglick River. The reason for the move is that ocean storm surges have begun flooding parts of the village that were once protected by ice shelves and frozen ground. These natural barriers have recently begun melting due to warmer temperatures.

Stanley Tom, who is Yup'ik himself and a member of the Newtok Traditional Council, told CNN News, "We are seeing the erosion, flooding, and sinking of our village right now." Newtok may be one of the first indigenous communities in the world to go through a complete relocation in order to survive, but it probably won't be the last. According to CNN, the United Nations Intergovernmental Panel on Climate Change says that Newtok is "part of a growing climate change crisis that will displace 150 million people by 2050."

MAP OF AFRICA

◀ The Darfur region of Sudan is highlighted in green.

Long-simmering ethnic, political, and religious antagonisms are some of the most visible causes of the conflicts in Darfur and Sudan. In 2007, however, a study by the United Nations Environment Program (UNEP) said that environmental degradation caused by climate change is a major factor contributing to the violence and to the migrations in the region.

The study said that the region has seen steady increases in desertification—forest turning into desert—in the past four decades, plus a loss of more than 11 percent of forest cover since 1990.

As farms are being lost to desertification, people are less able to obtain the food they need and are moving into other areas, putting pressure on the land and water supply in those new areas to serve more and more people. As well, having greatly reduced forest cover means that people are less and less able to use wood for shelter and heat (used in cooking as well as for staying warm) meaning that competition for these resources has become fierce—and in many cases, very violent.

The Evacuation of the Carteret Islands

Clearly, conflicts and migrations on the level of what is happening in Sudan are serious outcomes of climate change. Even without the added factor of ethnic, religious, and political enmity, the continued increase of global warming, such as the world has seen in the past 20 years, makes climate migration a very real possibility for decades to come. In fact, one such migration has already begun in the 21st century.

The country of Papua New Guinea lies in the southwestern part of the Pacific Ocean. It is made up of several islands, one group of

▶ Refugees from Darfur at the Farchana Refugee Camp in Chad line-up from early in the morning to collect water from stand pipes provided by aid workers. Over 18,000 people live in the camp and water supplies are always low.

MAP OF PAPUA NEW GUINEA AND INSET THE CARTERET ISLANDS

which is called the Carteret Islands, about 0.4 square mile (one square km) in size. About 1,400 people practiced agriculture and fishing as their main means of subsistence on the islands until 2005, at least. At that point, widespread flooding had begun making the islands uninhabitable. People's homes and gardens were continually being washed away by high tides, rising sea levels, and even small tidal waves. Drinking water and crops were contaminated by salt water from the Pacific Ocean. As one islander described the situation to an Australian newspaper, "The wild taros, the greens, the breadfruit, they don't grow any more. We just got coconuts and, when we can catch them, fish. All the gardens are spoilt. When the high tide comes in, all the saltwater goes in the gardens."

The World's First "Environmental Refugees"

Residents of the islands, scientists, and non-governmental organizations (NGOs) have claimed that this flooding was being caused by global warming, although the Carteret Islanders' practice of using dynamite to blow up coral reefs and kill fish may have also contributed to the problem by reducing the coral barriers around the islands. In any case, many experts predicted that the islands would be under water by 2015.

In 2003, the government of Papua New Guinea allotted some funds to begin the evacuation of the islands, but efforts to remove the islanders have been hampered by lack of money. The plan is to gradually remove the entire population of the Carteret Islands by 2020—making it the first time in history that an entire group of islands will have been evacuated, most likely because of climate change. Most of the evacuated islanders will go to the area in and around Bougainville, a large island about 60 miles (100 km) away. With all this happening, and with what lies in store for the residents of the Carteret Islands, it is no surprise that newspapers and television stations have started calling the Carteret Islanders "the world's first environmental refugees."

Managing Global-Warming Migrations

The case of the Carteret Islanders might be seen as affecting only a small number of people in a remote part of the world. Given what is known about how serious climate change is, however, such an evacuation may be just the beginning of migrations caused by global warming. If this is the case, what can people around the world do to deal with these migrations, which could be on a much bigger scale than the example in the South Pacific?

The best way to handle migration caused by global warming is to deal with the root cause—that is, to work toward stopping climate change. Many governments and non-governmental organizations are working hard to get people to agree to use more sustainable energy sources such as the Sun, wind, and water. It is also important that people reduce electricity use, reuse and recycle products that take up a lot of energy to produce, and curb pollution. If, for example, greenhouse gas emissions can be reduced by using cleaner energy sources, this will help to halt global warming, reduce polar ice cap melting, and make situations like the one in the Carteret Islands less likely to occur.

Taking Steps: The Kyoto Treaty and Beyond

To help accomplish the goal of reducing global warming, many countries have signed the Kyoto Treaty, a multi-nation agreement in which countries promise to reduce their carbon dioxide emissions and greenhouse gas production. Countries that agree to the Kyoto Treaty have maximum emissions levels assigned to them and are penalized by even lower limits if they go beyond them. Developed and developing countries each have different responsibilities under the treaty.

Of course, combating climate change is a long-term battle that will take many years and require collaboration between countries around the world. So what can be done in the meantime to prepare for the fact that large groups of people will still have to migrate, based on climate-change factors?

▶ *The Thames Barrier was built to protect London from being flooded by an unusually high tide surging up the river from the ocean. The barrier control room is manned 24 hours a day and weather and tide warnings are constantly monitored.*

◄ Renewable, green energy sources:
• Homes fitted with rooftop solar panels. Solar panels use the Sun's power in two ways. Solar thermal systems heat water in pipes in the panels, while solar photovoltaic panels use special cells that react with sunlight to create electricity.
• Wind turbine engineers carry out maintenance work at a wind farm.
• A hydroelectric plant uses the energy of water as it tumbles from a reservoir into the dam to spin turbine blades and generate electricity.

To that end, here are some questions governments, NGOs, and citizens will have to ask themselves:

• If people in one part of a country have to evacuate, what other parts of that country have space and facilities to take them in—perhaps on a permanent basis? In the example of Hurricane Katrina, plans were quickly made following the disaster to evacuate thousands of people to places outside of New Orleans, some of them as far away as Minneapolis, Chicago, and Milwaukee—all northern cities 1,000 miles (1,600 km) or more from New Orleans.

• What plans exist to repair damaged areas so that people who migrate away from them can return as quickly and safely as possible?

• What physical preparations can be made to make disasters caused by climate change less severe? For example, can barriers be erected to lessen the effect of a flood? The River Thames— a major river in the United Kingdom—has a huge barrier in place for just this reason (see left).

• In the event of a disaster, what plans are in place to help people caught in the affected area? For example, in an area prone to drought, what plans are there to bring in emergency food and water? One organization, the United Nations Convention to Combat Desertification (UNCCD) has developed a ten-year plan to prepare for droughts around the world—including how much food will be needed and what evacuation plans will need to be in place in a given area.

Please turn
off the
lights when
not in use

CHAPTER SIX

WHAT WILL THE FUTURE BRING?

Two major factors will affect human migration as we move deeper and deeper into the 21st century: climate change and globalization.

Reducing Carbon Footprints

The more companies look to "go global" and expand their businesses around the world, the greater the chances of contributing greenhouse gases, chemical pollutants, and toxic waste into the environment—and the greater chance of leaving what environmentalists call a larger "carbon footprint."

A carbon footprint is a measure of how much carbon dioxide a person, factory, or nation emits over a given time. Many companies around the

▲ Honda auto workers in Japan fit a hydrogen tank unit to the FCX Clarity fuel cell car. When hydrogen burns it releases energy to power the car, but no emissions—except water vapor!

◄ Every time we switch on an electric light, or travel in a car powered by gasoline, or use a product manufactured in a factory that uses a fossil fuel, we increase our carbon footprints.

world have adopted "green" strategies to reduce the size of their carbon footprints. These companies manufacture products or do business in ways that save energy, reduce waste, or take advantage of renewable energy. Many companies are concentrating on making products that function in ways that are more environmentally friendly when they are put to use. The electric car and the hydrogen fuel cell car are good examples of this kind of product.

Despite the commitment of some companies to help the environment in the manufacture and use of their products, the full-scale "greening" of global manufacturers is still a long way off. This is mainly because it is very expensive to switch over from the "old," large-carbon-footprint way of making things to a newer, greener one.

A Cycle of Globalization, Migration, and Global Warming?

As companies go global, they create more jobs and attract workers. As more workers and their families migrate to centers of business and industry, cities will grow and more people will build homes. This growth will create a demand for building services, cars, TVs, computers, and other items for people's homes. Factories and businesses will be built to provide these products and services. With the building of new homes, businesses, streets, neighborhoods, and the infrastructure to support them, will come a greater use of fuel and other energy sources.

▲ *A young ice-cream fan tastes an edible artwork displayed as part of a competition to find the next Ben & Jerry's "Do the world a flavor" fair trade ice-cream flavor. Fair trade products ensure that farmers and producers in developing countries use environmentally friendly farming practices and are paid a fair price for their produce. In addition to creating fair trade products, Ben & Jerry's cartons are made of cardboard from sustainable forests (forests in which new trees are planted when trees are felled), and they are developing freezers that use less energy and do not release gases that harm the ozone layer.*

Without greater efforts to reduce our carbon footprints, these activities will lead to increased levels of greenhouse gases and global warming. Many researchers predict that the environmental impact of higher temperatures—droughts, desertification, flooding, more severe weather—will create a new generation of climate migrants on a scale never before known to humankind. This pattern suggests that there is indeed some benefit to working harder to bring climate change, or global warming, under control for the sake of providing not just a cleaner, safer planet, but also a more stable way of life for generations to come.

Some Things to Think About

As the 21st century unfolds, here are some things to consider about how globalization and climate change are going to affect us all:

• According to a study from the United Nations University—a group that examines worldwide problems related to human survival and development—about 700 million people live at or just above sea level. In other words, one in every ten people on Earth may be in serious danger if sea levels rise significantly because of global warming. Some scientists estimate that by the end of the 21st century, sea levels could be over three feet (1 m) higher than they are today—

causing floods, storm surges—when strong winds ahead of a storm push on the water, creating huge tides that flood the land—and the migration of millions of people in coastal cities around the world.

• The Internet has made it easier for people to get information about other countries. This can increase the desire to migrate because it provides a "window" on other parts of the world. Since the Internet also makes it easier to connect with friends and families, however, it may make migration less necessary. Going online also makes it possible to conduct all kinds of business transactions at great distances, reducing the

◄ *Many workers can do their jobs using a computer in their own homes. They can stay in touch with colleagues without the need to travel to an office, and they can do business around the world without increasing their carbon footprints.*

amount of money needed to travel, and the amount of pollution caused by traveling from one place to another.

• Today, much of the work people used to do in offices can be done from home or other places that are not physically located at a company's home base. If a computer and a telephone are all people need to do their jobs, perhaps the need to migrate to "where the jobs are" will be much less in coming years.

• Many people oppose globalization because they believe that large, international companies will spread their products to so many countries that the people there will adopt them as "global brands" while forgetting about their own cultures. Think about Coca-Cola and McDonald's as just two of these global products—you can find both in many countries around the world. Will globalization make our world a better place because sharing these brands will help cultures mix? Or will groups fight to retain their identities?

◄ *The tiny island country of Tuvalu in the Pacific Ocean sits just 15 feet (4.5 m) above sea level. High tides are regularly flooding the island, while increased storm activity is creating wave erosion—the country is slowly being washed away.*

▼ *In Chongqing, China, the traditional Coca-Cola Santa stands beneath a 79-foot-tall (24-m-tall) christmas tree made from Coke cans. Many western celebrations, such as Christmas, Valentine's Day, and Halloween, are becoming popular with young people in China.*

▼ Children line up for a meal at the Gaushala camp for flood refugees in the Bihar province of India. In 2007, this region was just one area affected by extreme flooding during the monsoon season. Thousands of villages and farms were submerged in India, Bangladesh, and Nepal. In the Bihar province hundreds were killed and two million people were forced to evacuate to higher ground.

• Our supply of non-renewable energy from fossil fuels such as coal and oil is becoming scarcer. This has led to more and more people and communities taking responsibility for living a more "green" life by eating only locally grown food, that reduces pollution caused by transportation, and building energy-efficient homes and office buildings. It could also lead to a whole new way of thinking about where people want to move and settle. For example, a community committed to "green" living may decide that it is a good idea to move to a spot where there is more access to wind or wave power.

These are just some of the scenarios to keep in mind when thinking about how human migration patterns may develop in the 21st century. Given what is known about human history, it seems clear that people will continue to migrate for all kinds of reasons. Climate change and globalization are two reasons that will continue to be significant in the years to come.

WIND FARMS:
FOR AND AGAINST

A wind farm is a collection of wind turbines grouped in the same location. The wind propels the turbines which then generate electricity. The electricity is collected and sent out to the power system in the area for transmission to homes, schools, businesses, and places of recreation. Large wind farms may have hundreds of turbines in operation.

It would seem as though people thinking about clean and renewable energy would also think seriously about moving to areas near wind farms to take advantage of this form of "green" power. In Ontario, Canada's most populous province, however, quite the opposite has happened.

That's because although there is general agreement that wind farms are excellent sources of clean energy among people in Ontario, there has been a backlash against actually having them located in people's immediate area. Some call this the "NIMBY" effect—"Not in My Back Yard." In other words, people are saying, "Sure, a large-scale project like a wind farm might seem like a great idea, as long as it is not built where I can see it every day."

In fact, in 2006, a large manufacturer of wind turbines that had contracted with the Ontario government to build them announced that it was canceling construction of a large, 11-turbine facility because of public opposition. People said they did not want the farm built at a community on the shores of Lake Huron for a number of reasons that included opposition to the turbines' noise, their danger to bird populations, and the claim that they were spoiling the rural landscape and property values.

" None of us wants to have the transmission lines or the wires or generation sources close to home. (But) people have got to start asking themselves some pretty serious questions about this. . . At the end of the day, remember if we don't get these things up and sited, we're not going to have enough power. These (wind turbines) produce greener power, cleaner power, and we all have to do our bit."

Dwight Duncan, Ontario's Energy Minister

GLOSSARY

atmosphere The mass of gases surrounding Earth

climate change The overall change in Earth's climate, over time. In recent years, "climate change" has come to refer to the warming of Earth's average annual temperature and the term is often used along with "global warming"

climate migrant A person who has had to leave his or her home, or has chosen to leave their home, because of sudden or progressive changes in the environment that adversely affect their lives or living conditions. Climate migrants may move away temporarily or permanently, and their migration may be within their own country or to another country

drought A period of lower-than-normal rainfall over a given timespan. Droughts can often lead to the deaths of large numbers of people, animals, and plants as water in a region dries up

glacier A large ice mass that moves slowly over land

global warming A gradual rise in temperatures which is being caused by greenhouse gases trapping too much heat in Earth's atmosphere

globalization Growth on a worldwide scale in areas such as business or transportation. Globalized companies do business and hire employees around the world

greenhouse gases Gases such as carbon dioxide, nitrous oxide, or methane that are released into Earth's atmosphere when fossil fuels are burned

human rights The basic freedoms that all humans expect. These include the right to life, liberty, freedom of expression, and freedom of movement

infrastructure The basic system of organization or structures, such as utilities, roads, or buildings, required for the operation of a society

migration The movement of large numbers of people or animals from one place to another

monsoon A wind system in Asia that often brings heavy rains and can be extremely dangerous to life and property

Non-Governmental Organizations (NGOs) A non-profit, voluntary organization that does not have formal ties to local, regional, or national governments. NGOs usually work for human-rights or developmental causes

ozone layer A zone located about 9 to 30 miles (15 to 50 km) above Earth, that contains enough ozone (a form of oxygen) to block out most ultraviolet rays from the Sun

persecution The inflicting of pain, suffering, or harm on someone, especially for reasons of racial, religious, or ethnic background

polar ice caps A layer of ice that sits at the poles of a planet. In the case of Earth, both the South and North Poles have ice caps

pollution The contamination of air, water, or soil by harmful substances, such as greenhouse gases, oil, chemicals, or trash

storm surge A rise in water levels on large bodies of water caused by the pressure of high winds, commonly found in large storms such as cyclones or hurricanes

United Nations An organization started in 1945 and made up of most of the world's countries that promotes international peace and security

World Bank An agency created by the United Nations to help developing countries by loaning them money from other member nations

IDEAS FOR DISCUSSION

- *Which organizations have you seen fighting against climate change in your region? What things have you done to help in the fight against climate change? Can you give some examples of companies or other organizations that are contributing to the problem of climate change in your region or country?*

- *What examples of globalized companies are operating in your area? Can you see any differences between the way these companies operate in comparison to businesses that only operate locally? Do you think any of these differences are contributing to climate change, or helping combat climate change?*

- *Has your own family, or the family of a friend or classmate been part of a migration? What were the historical details behind that migration?*

- *What predictions would you make about how climate change and globalization will affect where you live in the next 10 or 20 years?*

- *Have you or your family or friends ever considered or talked about migrating in the future? What are some of the factors that might be behind such a move?*

FURTHER INFORMATION

www.iom.int
The International Organization for Migration (IOM) was established in 1951 and has 127 member states and offices in more than one hundred countries. It works with governments, NGOs, and other groups and is "dedicated to promoting humane and orderly migration for the benefit of all." The IOM provides services to governments and migrants in pursuit of this aim.

www.un.org/esa/population/migration
United Nations – International Migration and Development: This division of the United Nations is devoted to migration and development around the world, and its home page contains links to international reports, publications and global forums, as well as a comprehensive list of links to other migration groups around the world.

www.davidsuzuki.org/Climate_Change
The David Suzuki Foundation, headed by the world-famous Canadian environmental scientist, has a comprehensive page on climate change on its Web site.

www.globalization101.org
Managed by the Levin Foundation, this site provides an excellent overview of all of the major components of globalization—and it is especially geared toward students!

INDEX

INDEX

ABOUT THE AUTHOR

Paul Challen has written several nonfiction books for both adults and young readers on topics that include science, history, sports, biographies, and entertainment. His books have been translated into several languages, and he has also written widely for radio, magazines, and newspapers.